Holiday Cooking for Kids!

THANKSGIVING
Sweets and Treats

By Ronne Randall

WINDMILL BOOKS

New York

Published in 2013 by Windmill Books, An Imprint of Rosen Publishing
29 East 21st Street, New York, NY 10010

First Edition

Produced for Windmill by Ruby Tuesday Books Ltd
Editor for Ruby Tuesday Books Ltd: Mark J. Sachner
US Editor: Sara Antill
Designer: Emma Randall

Photo Credits:

Cover, 1, 3, 4–5, 6–7, 8–9, 10–11, 12 (bottom), 13, 14, 15 (top), 16–17, 18–19, 21, 22, 23 (top), 24, 26–27, 28–29, 30–31 © Shutterstock; 12 (top) © Wikipedia (public domain); 15 (bottom), 20, 23 (bottom), 25 © Ruby Tuesday Books Ltd.

Library of Congress Cataloging-in-Publication Data

Randall, Ronne.
Thanksgiving sweets and treats / by Ronne Randall.
    p. cm. — (Holiday cooking for kids!)
 Includes index.
 ISBN 978-1-4488-8082-9 (library binding) — ISBN 978-1-4488-8129-1 (pbk.) —
ISBN 978-1-4488-8135-2 (6-pack)
1. Thanksgiving cooking—Juvenile literature. I. Title.
TX739.2.T45R36 2013
641.5—dc23
                                    2012006774

Manufactured in the United States of America

CPSIA Compliance Information: Batch #B3S12WM: For Further Information contact Windmill Books, New York, New York at 1-866-478-0556

Contents

A Festival of Food and Fun

In 1620, the **Pilgrims** landed at Plymouth Harbor, in what would later become Massachusetts. They faced many hardships and barely survived their first winter. But with the help of the native Wampanoag people, they planted crops and enjoyed a plentiful **harvest** in the fall of 1621. To give thanks for their good fortune, they held a three-day feast and invited their Wampanoag neighbors. There are no records of what was served at this first Thanksgiving dinner, but it probably included wild turkeys, corn, squash, pumpkin, and wild cranberries.

Thanksgiving was celebrated on different days in different parts of America until 1863, when President Abraham Lincoln made the fourth Thursday in November a national holiday of Thanksgiving. Americans have celebrated on that day ever since.

Today, most Thanksgiving meals feature the now-traditional turkey, cranberry sauce, pumpkin pie, corn, mashed potatoes, and sweet potatoes.

The recipes in this book will give you some tasty and fun ways to add to your own Thanksgiving feast!

Before you start cooking, check out all the tips and information on the following pages.

Get Ready to Cook

- Wash your hands using soap and hot water. This will help to keep bacteria away from your food.
- Make sure the kitchen countertop and all your equipment is clean.
- Read the recipe carefully before you start cooking. If you don't understand a step, ask an adult to help you.
- Gather all the ingredients and equipment you will need.

Safety First!

It's very, very important to have an adult around whenever you do any of the following tasks in the kitchen:

1. Operating machinery or turning on kitchen appliances such as a mixer, food processor, blender, stovetop burners, or the oven.

2. Using sharp utensils, such as knives, can openers, or vegetable peelers.

3. Working with hot pots, pans, or cookie sheets.

Electric hand mixer

Knife

Saucepan

Wooden spoon

Cutting board

You will need these kitchen utensils to make the recipes in this book.

Vegetable peeler

Whisk

Oven mitt

Rolling pin

Kettle

Colander

Cookie sheet

Measuring Counts!

Measure your ingredients carefully. If you get a measurement wrong, it could affect how successful your dish turns out to be. Measuring cups and spoons are two of the most important pieces of equipment in a kitchen.

Measuring Cups

Measuring cups are used to measure the volume, or amount, of liquid or dry ingredients. Measuring cups usually hold from 1 cup to 4 cups. If you have a 1-cup measuring cup, that should be fine for all the recipes in this book. Measuring cups have markings on them that show how many cups or parts of a cup you are measuring.

Measuring Spoons

Like measuring cups, measuring spoons are used to measure the volume of liquid or dry ingredients, only in smaller amounts. Measuring spoons come in sets with different spoons for teaspoons, tablespoons, and smaller parts.

Measuring spoons

Cooking Techniques

Here are some tasks that anyone who is following directions for cooking should be sure to understand.

Bringing to a boil

Heating a liquid or mixture in a saucepan on the stovetop until it is bubbling.

Simmering

First bringing a liquid or mixture to a boil, and then turning down the heat so it's just at or below the boiling point and the bubbling has nearly stopped.

Preheating

Heating the oven until it has reached the temperature required for the recipe.

All of these tasks require the use of heat, so you should be absolutely sure to have an adult around when you do them.

Apple-Honey Cranberry Sauce

Because cranberry sauce goes so well with turkey, it's become as much a part of Thanksgiving dinner as the turkey itself.

Cranberry plants grow on wet, soft ground in fields known as bogs. At harvest time, farmers flood the bogs with about 18 inches (46 cm) of water. Machinery loosens the ripe cranberries from the plants so that they float to the water's surface. Then the farmers can skim the berries off the water and collect them.

This recipe for luscious cranberry sauce uses apples, apple juice, and honey to give it sweetness, and **spices** to give it a bit of zing. Yum!

You will need – ingredients:

4 cups cranberries, fresh or frozen

1 large sweet apple

2 cups apple juice or sweet apple cider

1 teaspoon ground cinnamon

½ teaspoon ground ginger

1 cup honey

Thanksgiving Food Facts

Nutritionists have long thought that raw cranberries have a wide range of health benefits. They are high in antioxidants, which help the body fight heart disease and other ailments. Scientists are also studying how cranberries might help our bodies fight various infections, blood clotting, and cancer. Cranberries are also high in **fiber**, which helps us digest our food!

You will need – equipment:

Vegetable peeler

Knife

Saucepan

Wooden spoon

Potholder or oven mitt for handling saucepan

Step-by-Step:

Remember to ask an adult for help when you are using the vegetable peeler, the knife, and the stove.

1. Peel and core the apple, then chop into tiny pieces.

2. Put apple juice, chopped apple, and spices into the saucepan.

3. Bring the mixture to a boil.

4. When the mixture is boiling, add the cranberries and honey, stirring gently with the wooden spoon.

5. Reduce the heat and simmer, stirring often, until the mixture turns into a deep red sauce. This should take about 20–30 minutes.

6. Let the sauce cool and serve with turkey.

Thanksgiving Food Facts

Cranberries grew wild in the American Northeast, and the Native Americans of the region used them to make dye for cloth as well as for food. They mixed cranberries with deer meat to make a high-energy food called pemmican, which they took with them on long hunting trips. Cranberries are pretty sour in their natural state, so the Pilgrims and early settlers probably sweetened theirs with maple sugar.

Super Simple Succotash

Corn and beans, the main ingredients of succotash, were grown by Native Americans who lived in New England, and it's very likely that a version of succotash was served at the first Thanksgiving. It's been a traditional part of Thanksgiving dinner ever since.

Succotash contains lots of healthy fiber, which makes it filling and very good for you!

This is The First Thanksgiving at Plymouth *by artist Jennie A. Brownscombe. It was painted in 1914.*

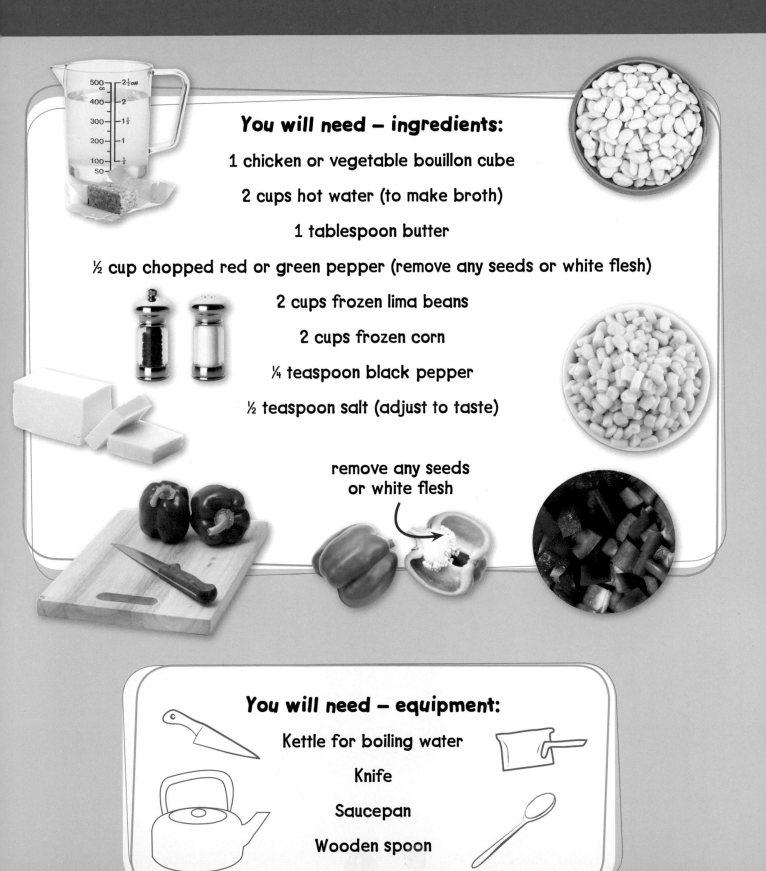

You will need – ingredients:

1 chicken or vegetable bouillon cube

2 cups hot water (to make broth)

1 tablespoon butter

½ cup chopped red or green pepper (remove any seeds or white flesh)

2 cups frozen lima beans

2 cups frozen corn

¼ teaspoon black pepper

½ teaspoon salt (adjust to taste)

remove any seeds
or white flesh

You will need – equipment:

Kettle for boiling water

Knife

Saucepan

Wooden spoon

Step-by-Step:

Remember to ask an adult for help when you are using the knife and the stove.

1. Make two cups of chicken or vegetable broth by dissolving the bouillon cube in boiling water.

2. Heat and melt the butter in the saucepan. Then add the chopped pepper.

3. Cook for a minute or two, until the pepper pieces are soft. Stir them every few seconds to stop them from sticking to the saucepan.

4. Add the broth, lima beans, and corn to the pan, and stir.

5. Bring to a boil.

6. Lower the heat and simmer until the corn and lima beans are tender, about 15 or 20 minutes.

7. Add salt and pepper and stir.

8. When it's cool enough to eat, put it on your Thanksgiving table and enjoy!

When the butter looks like this, it's time to add the chopped pepper.

14

Thanksgiving Food Facts

Corn is native to the Americas and was grown by the ancient Indians of Mexico almost 10,000 years ago! The Taino Indians of the Caribbean called it mahiz, and corn is still called maize in some parts of the world today.

Pumpkin Pie

No Thanksgiving dinner is complete without pie for dessert, and pumpkin pie is one of the most popular.

The pumpkin is a fruit. In fact, it is the world's largest fruit! Pumpkins belong to the same family as squashes and melons. The meaty part that we use in making pumpkin pie is the shell of the fruit.

If you use a ready-made, unbaked pie shell, pumpkin pie is also easy to make! Here's how to mix up a perfect pie to top off your perfect Thanksgiving dinner.

You will need – ingredients:

15 ounce (425 g) can of pureed pumpkin

1 cup granulated sugar

½ teaspoon salt

2 teaspoons ground cinnamon

1 teaspoon ground ginger

¼ teaspoon ground cloves

2 eggs

12 ounce (355 ml) can of evaporated milk

1 deep, unbaked 9 inch (23 cm) pie shell

You will need – equipment:

Small mixing bowl

Large mixing bowl

Whisk or eggbeater

Wooden spoon

Potholder or oven mitt for handling pie in oven

Toothpick

Step-by-Step:

Remember to ask an adult for help when you are using the stove.

1. Preheat the oven to 425°F (215°C).

2. Mix the sugar, salt, cinnamon, ginger, and cloves in the small bowl.

3. Use the whisk or eggbeater to beat the eggs in the large bowl.

4. Stir the pumpkin and sugar and spice mixture into the beaten egg.

5. Gradually stir in the evaporated milk. Stir until everything is well combined and smooth.

6. Pour the mixture into the pie shell.

7. Bake in the preheated oven for 15 minutes.

8. Reduce the oven temperature to 350°F (175°C) and bake for another 40–50 minutes.

9. To test whether the pie is done, insert a toothpick near the center of the pie. If it comes out clean, it's done. If some mixture is sticking to it, bake for another 5 minutes and test again.

10. Serve warm (not straight from the oven, though!) with ice cream, or cool with whipped cream. Either way, it's a dessert worth giving thanks for!

Pumpkin flowers

Pumpkin seeds

Thanksgiving Food Facts

Like other fruits, pumpkins have flowers and seeds. The flowers grow for a very short time on the pumpkin vine. Most of us are familiar with the seeds, which we find inside pumpkins when we carve jack-o'-lanterns at Halloween. Both the flowers and seeds of a pumpkin are edible. Pumpkin flowers are used for food in a variety of ways. Some people use them in salads, and they may even be fried in oil or deep fried, like zucchini strips! Pumpkin seeds are a popular snack, especially when they are roasted and salted.

Gobblin' Good Cookies

Here's another kind of Thanksgiving turkey to enjoy! Wow your family and friends with these sweet turkey-shaped cookie treats at snack time. They're a great way to use up any candy corn you might have left over from Halloween. And because they're made from your own handprints, they'll really have that personal touch!

Thanksgiving Food Facts

The Pilgrims probably brought cookies to America, but they would have called them "jumbles." These were small cakes made of nuts, flour, eggs, sugar, and spices. The word "cookie" came with the Dutch settlers who arrived later on. "Koekje" means "little cake" in Dutch.

You will need – ingredients:

½ cup (1 stick) butter, softened

¼ cup sugar

1 small egg

1 teaspoon vanilla extract

1½ cups all-purpose flour

¼ teaspoon baking powder

Candy corn

Ready-to-use decorating icing tubes in red, yellow, brown, and any other colors you like

Baking Powder

You will need – equipment:

Large mixing bowl

Electric hand mixer

Plastic wrap

Rolling pin

Clean, flat surface for rolling out dough

Sturdy cardboard

Pencil

Scissors

Small knife

Circular cookie cutters

Cookie sheet

Potholder or oven mitt for handling cookie sheet

Step-by-Step:

Remember to ask an adult for help when you are using the electric hand mixer, knife, and oven.

1. Using the electric mixer, beat the butter and sugar together until creamy, then add the egg and vanilla extract and beat until well blended.

2. Gradually add the flour and baking powder, and beat until it's just blended.

3. Shape the dough into a ball, wrap in plastic wrap, and cool in the refrigerator for an hour or in the freezer for 30 minutes.

4. While the dough is cooling, trace your handprint onto the cardboard. Spread your fingers out wide, because the cookie dough will spread as it bakes.

5. Carefully cut out the handprint.

6. Preheat the oven to 350°F (175°C).

7. Place the chilled dough on a flat, lightly floured surface and roll out till it's about ¼ inch (8 mm) thick.

8. Place the cardboard handprint onto the dough and use the knife to carefully cut around the handprint to make as many cookies as you can.

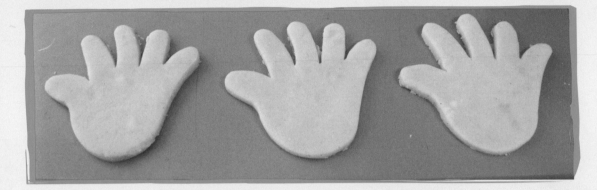

9. Alternatively, use a round large cookie cutter to cut circles of dough. For each large circle, cut a small circle, too.

10. Place the cookies about 1 inch (2.5 cm) apart on the cookie sheet and bake in the preheated oven for 10–12 minutes, or until lightly browned. Take out to cool.

11. When the cookies are cool, they're ready to decorate! Use the decorating icing on the handprint turkeys to make the turkey's tail feathers. Make its eyes and wattle with icing.

12. If you've made circular cookies, use some icing to stick a small cookie onto a large cookie. Then make the tail feathers using icing and candy corn. Decorate the turkey's face with icing or candy.

13. All you have to do now is gobble up these tasty gobblers!

Turkey Salad Mini Rolls

No matter how many people you share Thanksgiving dinner with, there is bound to be leftover turkey. Try using some of the leftovers to make these tasty mini sandwiches. They are a great snack to share with your friends over the holiday weekend!

You will need – ingredients:

1 cup leftover turkey meat, diced or shredded

2 tablespoons mayonnaise
(you can use more or less, depending on your own taste)

1½ tablespoons finely chopped apple

1½ tablespoons finely chopped celery

1 tablespoon dried, sweetened cranberries

8 mini burger buns, split in half

You will need – equipment:

Mixing bowl

Fork for mixing

Knife

Step-by-Step:

1. Mix the chopped turkey with the mayonnaise.

2. Add the apple, celery, and cranberries, and mix well.

3. Put sandwich filling on one side of each mini bun, top with the other half, and enjoy! Could anything be easier or more delicious?

Thanksgiving Food Facts

Ninety-one percent of the Americans surveyed by the National Turkey Federation eat turkey at Thanksgiving. Since the average Thanksgiving turkey weighs 15 pounds (6.8 kg), about 675 million pounds (305 million kg) of turkey is served on Thanksgiving Day. No wonder there are lots of leftovers!

Turkey Noodle Soup

Still have some leftover turkey? How about making a pot of steaming turkey noodle soup?

A comforting bowl of soup is the perfect way to warm up on a chilly November day. It's easy to make, nutritious, and delicious! It's so good that everyone will want some, so be prepared to share.

You will need – ingredients:

Large pot of salted water

1 quart (0.9 l) chicken stock
(can be made from 2 chicken bouillon cubes dissolved in 1 quart hot water)

4 ounces (113 g) egg noodles (or other pasta of your choice)
(Note: you may measure this amount by using about ¼ of a 16-ounce box
or bag of pasta)

¾ cup cooked turkey meat, diced

1 carrot, peeled and diced

1 celery stalk, diced

Salt and pepper to taste

1 tablespoon chopped parsley

You will need – equipment:

Stock pot or large saucepan

Vegetable peeler

Knife

Potholder or oven mitts for handling pot

Colander

Step-by-Step:

Remember to ask an adult for help when you are using the vegetable peeler, the knife, and the stove.

1. Bring the pot of salted water to a boil over medium heat.

2. Add the noodles to the boiling water, and cook according to the directions on the package.

3. When the noodles are cooked, drain in the colander and rinse with cold water. Set them aside.

4. Put the prepared chicken stock in the pot and simmer over medium heat. (Again, get an adult to help with this.)

5. Add the carrots and celery. Simmer until they are tender.

6. Season the stock with salt and pepper.

7. Add the cooked noodles and the turkey.

8. Simmer until they are heated all the way through.

9. Pour into bowls and decorate with chopped parsley. Your soup is ready to serve!

You can put skinny or wide egg noodles, macaroni, spaghetti, or any other kind of pasta into your turkey soup!

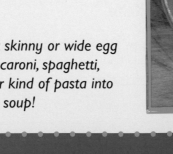

Thanksgiving Food Facts

Hot soup, like chicken soup and turkey soup, really does have healing powers! Scientists have discovered that eating hot soup when you have a cold can help reduce symptoms like a stuffy nose and sore throat. Plus, the soup is full of **vitamins** and minerals that will help you recover.

Thick and Tasty Pumpkin Smoothies

Here's another desserty dish that fits right into any Thanksgiving holiday menu—a batch of thick, sweet-tasting pumpkin smoothies. With their wonderful blend of flavors, they are kind of like a late-autumn milkshake, and they're good for you!

You will need – ingredients:

½ cup canned pureed pumpkin

1 cup vanilla yogurt

2 cups milk

½ teaspoon ground cinnamon

¼ teaspoon ground nutmeg

4 ice cubes

Added toppings for serving, such as whipped cream, shaved white or dark chocolate, sprinkles, cinnamon, or wafers

You will need – equipment:

Blender or food processor

Drinking glasses

Drinking straws

Step-by-Step:

Remember to ask an adult for help when you are using the food processor.

1. Combine the pumpkin, yogurt, milk, cinnamon, nutmeg, and ice cubes in food processor or blender.

2. Blend until all the ice is chopped and the ingredients are smooth and creamy

3. Pour into glasses and serve immediately with drinking straws. If you really want to make these a festive treat, try serving them in fancy dessert or drinking glasses!

4. To add more sweetness, flavor, and color, put a little whipped cream or whipped topping, shaved chocolate, a pinch of cinnamon, or some colored sprinkles on top. You can even add a sweet, crispy wafer to scoop it all up with!

Glossary

fiber (FY-ber) A substance found in celery, cereals, and other plants that the human body can't break down and that helps move food through our digestive systems.

harvest (HAR-vist) The picking, collecting, or cutting down of fruits, vegetables, and grain crops when they are ripe and ready for eating.

nutritionists (noo-TRIH-shun-ists) People who are experts in how to provide food that is necessary to our health and growth.

Pilgrims (PIL-grumz) Members of a group who came to America from England in search of religious freedom and founded the Plymouth Colony in present-day Massachusetts in 1620.

spices (SPYS-ez) Substances usually made from dried seeds, roots, or other parts of plants that provide foods with specific aromas and flavors.

vitamins (VY-tuh-minz) Substances found in foods that are needed by the body for health and growth.

Index

Websites

For web resources related to the subject of this book, go to: www.windmillbooks.com/weblinks and select this book's title.